FROG
MOVES OUT
of the RAIN FOREST

by Nikki Potts

illustrated by Maarten Lenoir

PICTURE WINDOW BOOKS
a capstone imprint

The air is warm.
Food is plentiful.
The neighbors are nice.

It's the rain forest, and it's
where Frog calls home.

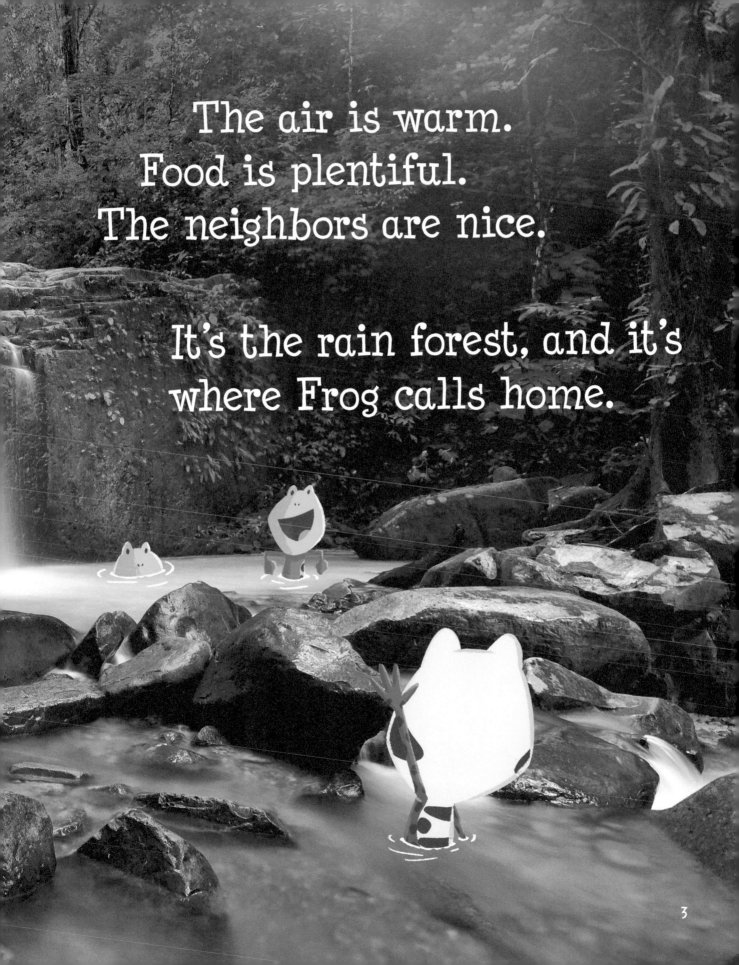

But Frog knows there is much more to the world, and she is going to see it all!

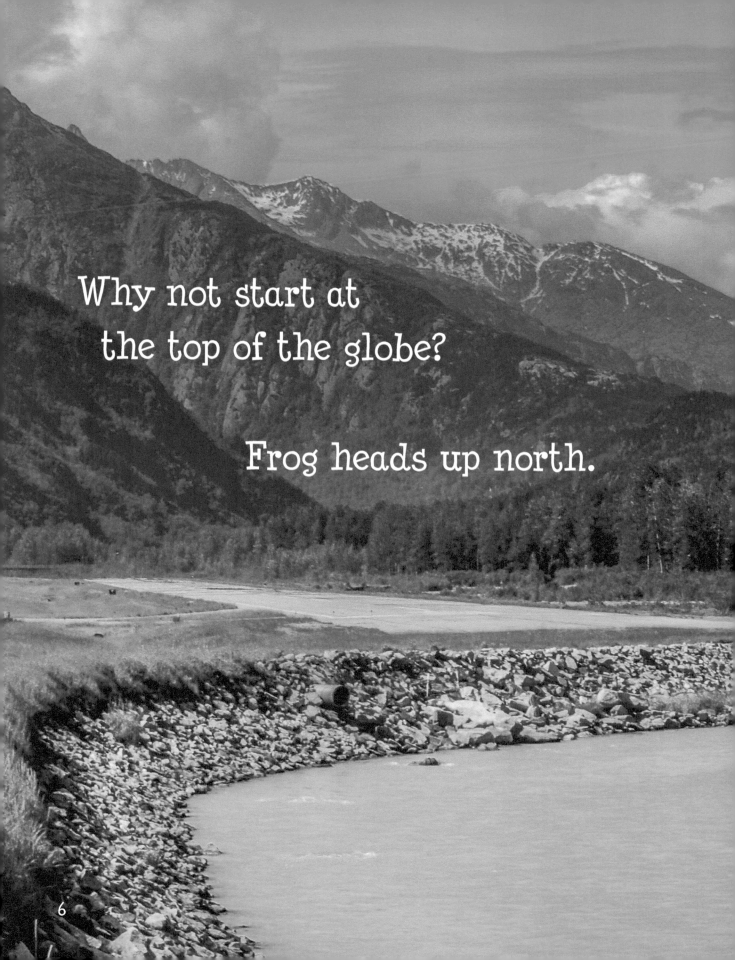

Why not start at
the top of the globe?

Frog heads up north.

The trees remind her of the rain forest.

Exploring the wilderness
has always been on
Frog's to-do list.

Who doesn't love
a good adventure?

This is NOT the kind of
adventure Frog was imagining.

The great outdoors
isn't as great as she
thought it was.

Frog needs to
find somewhere
with fewer fish.

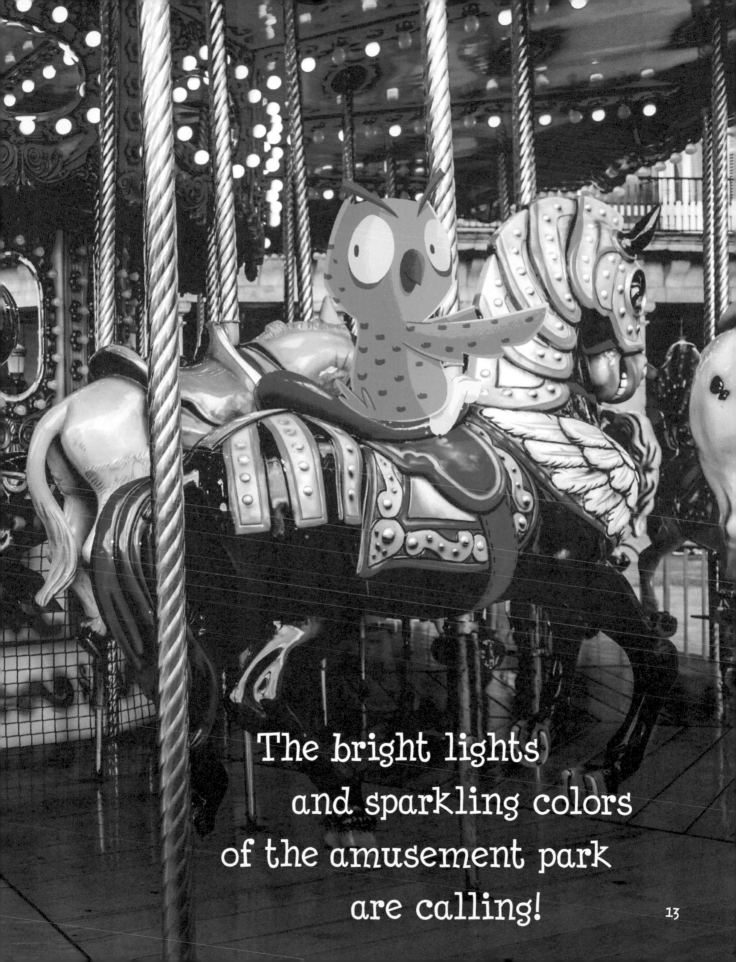

The bright lights
and sparkling colors
of the amusement park
are calling!

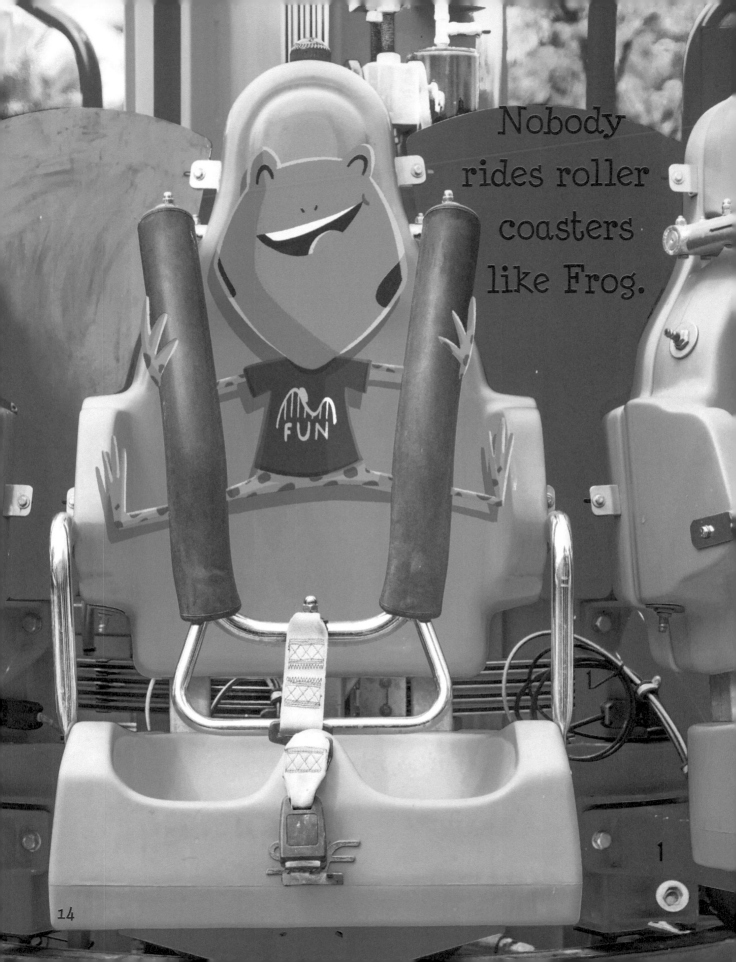

Nobody rides roller coasters like Frog.

Sticky feet help Frog feel safe—but still scared!—on even the loopiest loops.

Frog has ridden every carnival ride there is to ride.

It is time to say goodbye to the park.

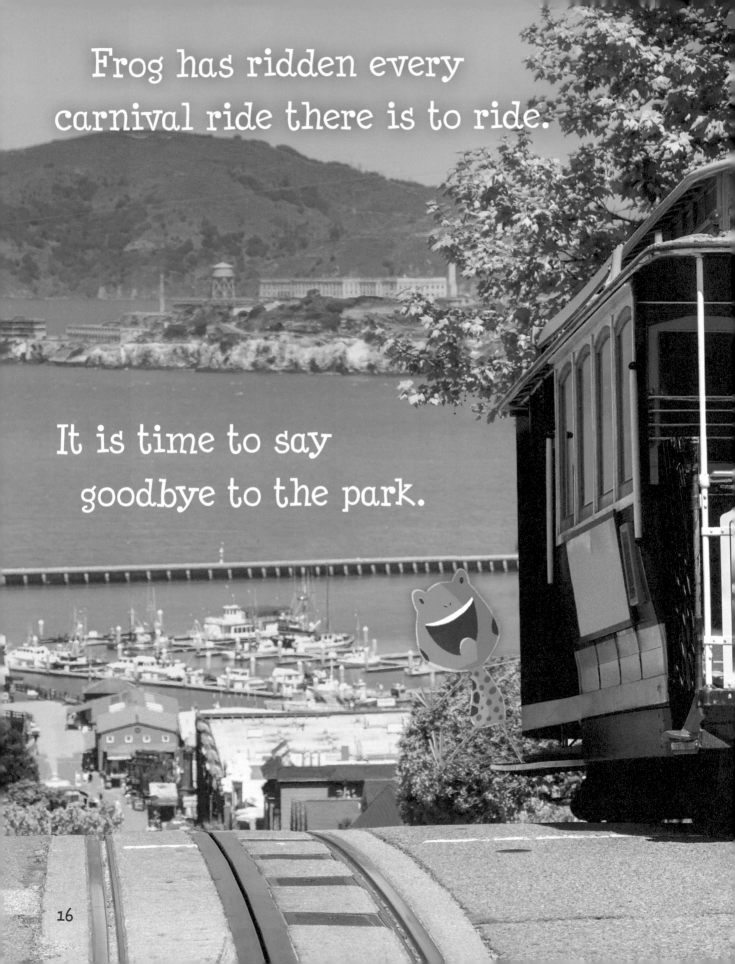

Off to the next adventure!

Frog has always wanted
to paint from the top
of a mountain.

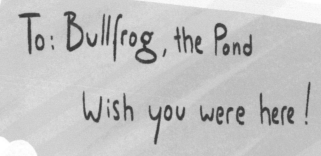

To: Bullfrog, the Pond

Wish you were here!

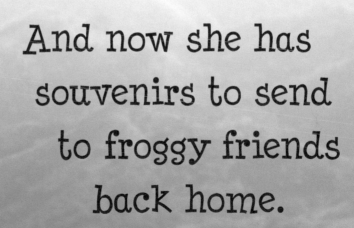

And now she has
souvenirs to send
to froggy friends
back home.

Across the globe,
Frog is feeling important.

Where else would
she find statues
of herself?

The Eiffel Tower gives Frog
a great view of the city.

Wow!
She has never seen
anything like it.

The giant sequoia trees
are tall too.

Frog feels very small.

So much has been seen and
done during Frog's world tour.

But Frog is
homesick.

It's time for
vacation to end.

Every place Frog
visited was amazing.
But now Frog is ready
to rest—at least for
a little while!

The rain forest
really is the perfect
place for Frog to
call home.

MORE ABOUT POISON DART FROGS

Females leave their tadpoles in spiky tropical plants called bromeliads.

Poison dart frogs are toxic enough to kill. The toxins in their bodies come from the food they eat.

Poison dart frogs do not have webbing between their toes. This means they are not good swimmers.

Poison dart frogs can be one of many bright colors or a combination of colors.

Poison dart frogs catch bugs with their long sticky tongues.

ANIMAL PASSPORT

Name: Poison Dart Frog

Type: amphibian

Habitat: rain forest

Diet: carnivorous; they eat insects and invertebrates

Size: 1 inch (2.54 centimeters)

Weight: 1 ounce (.03 kilograms)

Lifespan: 3 to 15 years

Favorite Activity: climbing

BOOKS IN THIS SERIES

Habitat Hunter is published by Picture Window Books, an imprint of Capstone.
1710 Roe Crest Drive
North Mankato, Minnesota 56003
www.capstonepub.com

**Library of Congress Cataloging-in-Publication Data is available
on the Library of Congress website.**
ISBN: 978-1-9771-1423-5 (library binding)
ISBN: 978-1-9771-2021-2 (paperback)
ISBN: 978-1-9771-1429-7 (eBook PDF)

Summary: Frog is bored with their habitat! Follow Frog as they try out different places to live. Which habitat will make the best home for Frog?

Image Credits
Shutterstock: anek.soowannaphoom, cover, 1, bancika, 22-23, Bonita R. Chester, 8-9, Curioso, 12-13, Dirk Ercken, 31, gowithstock, 14, Logra, 24-25, lunamarina, 16-17, My Life Graphic, 18-19, nelik, 26-27, Nokuro, 2-3, Paul Winterman, 10-11, RoD7, 4-5, Sabaidee, 28-29, SIHASAKPRACHUM, 15, Somporn Wongvichienkul, 20-21, Stephanie Michelle 82, 6-7

Artistic elements: Shutterstock: pingebat, Valeriya_Dor

Editorial Credits
Editor: Mari Bolte; Designer: Kayla Rossow; Media Researcher: Kelly Garvin;
Production Specialist: Tori Abraham

All internet sites appearing in back matter were available
and accurate when this book was sent to press.